A Song of Ireland

A Collection of Poems

Sinéad Tyrone

ISBN: 978-0-9984018-7-4

A Song of Ireland/Tyrone-1st ed.
1. Poems. 2. Poetry. 3. Verse.
4. Ireland. 5. Irish Heritage. 6. Tyrone

Cover and interior photos by Sinéad Tyrone
Cover design by Beth Bales Ostrowski

NFB/Amelia Press
<<◇>>
119 Dorchester Road
Buffalo, New York 14213
For more information please visit
nfbpublishing.com

To Beth, my artist, my treasured friend.
Thank you for helping my dreams of Ireland come true.

Also by Sinéad Tyrone

Walking Through The Mist (fiction)

Crossing The Lough Between (fiction)

Fragility (poetry)

The Poems

Donegal Castle Ghosts
Transfixed At Slieve League
Cara Na Mara, Magheraclogher
Crossing Derryveagh Mountains
Fine Mist, Clearing
Two Cottages
Five Hundred Ploughs
Blue Stack Mountain Pass
Grianan At Night
Song For Derry
Bloody Sunday Revisited
Bishop Street Without
A Gathering of Friends
Other End Of The Bridge
White Wine and Smiles
Soft Days
Crossing Carrick-a-Rede
Lost in Mussenden Temple
Causeway Reflection
Ravens Circling Overhead
Fair Head Light
A Song of Ireland
Ireland Dawn
Upon Leaving Dublin

Upon Leaving Killyleagh

Your last look at Killyleagh
as your boat pulled away from harbor,
as you cast your sight one final time
on its seaside cottages,
and the hills beyond,

Did tears form in your eyes
as your heart, broken,
bade farewell to familiar faces,
as your roots yanked free
of their ground?

Or did you turn a blind eye,
heart as cold and hard
as the wind whipped waves
that buffeted your craft?

For some,
escaping extreme poverty,
crushing prejudice,
unrequited hope,
cared little for the land they left behind,

While others would forever grieve
the home they were forced to flee.

And what of you?
As Killyleagh became a speck on the horizon,
as hills faded into oblivion
did you cry for what lie behind?
Or harden your heart to the past
and look forward?

Circle Completed

Empty cottages mark my passing,
roofs long ago collapsed,
stone walls crumbling in various degrees,
empty yards surround them,
weeds and ivy encroaching
where gardens once thrived.
I drive narrow roads,
note abandoned cottages,
feel the pull of their former inhabitants,
as I feel the pull of my own ancestors
long ago emigrated to a land
they hoped would be gold,
the color of freedom, the color of wealth.
One hundred fifty years they've been gone
from this land of green,
I cannot really lay claim to its history,
I am not truly part of its hills and loughs,
castles and crosses,
yet the drop of my blood that is connected
to the blood of my ancestors burns hot
as I drive through counties
whose names whisper on the wind like magic,
Wicklow, Kerry, Tipperary,
as I enter the north,
Antrim, Tyrone, Donegal,
their names breathe life into my soul,
set my heart to dancing,
anchor me to the land,
connect me through invisible bonds
to its people, its language, its stories.
I return to my ancestral village,
complete the circle of the journey
my forbears set out on,
feel peace in my heart
as I finally reach the place where I belong.

Dublin Shadows

You are here,
mixed with the crowds
of tourists and shoppers
that clog Dublin streets,
invisible presence
swirling wherever I walk.
I see you at the GPO
where the Proclamation was read,
feel you in St. Stephen's Green
where your blood mingled
with grass and early flowers,
imagine you marching down O'Connell Street
towards your doom.

I think of you at Dublin Castle,
how surprised the ruling party was
that you managed to hold it so long.

I weep for you at Kilmainham
as I walk past your cells
and the executioner's courtyard,
picture your blood staining stones,
your brave demeanor as
the final shots rang loud.

I trace the bullet hole
still evident in the GPO,
whisper another prayer
that your spirits now rest in peace.

Lost Between Kells and Long Library

Beyond the grand display
portraying how the Book of Kells
was created and survived

how the paper was made
how the color dyes were developed
and the pens were crafted

what life was like for the monks
who drew such fanciful images
who protected their treasure

beyond all of that
before the steps that lead up
to the Long Library

Mecca to readers
floor to ceiling bookshelves
housing rarest original manuscripts

grand room so holy
feet tipoe, fingers reach with trepidation
voices held at whisper

sandwiched between
historical display
and historical archives

in a plain glass case
is the Book of Kells
smaller than one would expect

miraculous in its existence
ornate page displaying
painstaking elaborate craft

in the *other* corner of the case
the one you would ignore
if you did not know

sits a writing
in His own hands
St. Patrick himself

and this writing
this letter
makes Him real

thrills my soul
sends tingling exhilaration
along my arms and legs

imagination grasping the concrete
heart pounding
blood racing

This is the treasure I sought
more magnificent than Kells
more powerful than ancient manuscripts

how many have missed this
how many have not known
their eyes fixed on other jewels

I gaze at letter
fragile paper
fragile writing

hard to believe
I am seeing
what He Himself touched

Grafton Street Flowers

Brick buildings rise high
on either side of street,
mix with concrete road,
blend with pale grey sky
all washed with the day's drizzle

I turn a corner and spot her,
middle aged woman
surrounded by every color of spring flower
there could be,
pinks and purples, corals and blues,
each group separated by paper,
brightest light on the street

If I hadn't been traveling,
if I could have kept them
safe and fresh
I would have bought an armful
of the brilliant treasures she sold,
would have thought of her all night
as they graced my dining room table.

Gold for the Gods

Visualize your skilled hands
forming molds for benches,
miniature oars,

melting and pouring
liquid gold for them
and for the hull,

how hard your heart
must have beat inside
your chest as you fitted each,

connecting them
with delicate maneuvers,
affixing wire thin mast

Intricate work created
with utmost care
for the sea god whose protection you sought.

I have no sea god
to call upon,
to fear,

the mechanics of my faith
so different,
so far removed from yours,

I offer my being
instead of hand fashioned gifts
meant to appease and please,

Yet through museum display glass
I can feel the pull of
gold boat's magic

marvel at the mastery of your work
and know your sea god
must have been well pleased.

Eyes Fixed on Distant Glory

There it was,
shining just beyond the horizon,
so close they could almost touch it,
still just beyond reach,
calling them to seek her out,

And answer her call they did,
poets and visionaries,
taste of freedom tantalizing to their tongues,
quickening their pulses,
racing their heartbeats,

They dreamed,
they dared to hope,
they made plans,

Eyes fixed on distant glory
their countrymen could not yet see,
so downtrodden after centuries of foreign occupation,
so consumed with providing daily food and shelter.

A few brave, young souls
caught the vision,
so very few against the large royal battalion,

Gathering courage they followed their dream-led leaders,
outstretched hands
grasping at unattainable treasure.

They fell.

Yet in their falling they succeeded,
seeds planted in freshly plowed soil,
springing forth in due season.

Glory now shines across their land,
yet every so often,
when the air stirs just right,
those whose eyes were so fixed
as to fight for an impossible cause
are remembered with tearful eyes
and grateful hearts.

Whispers Inside Jerpoint Walls

Stone walls,
what's left of them,
tower so high overhead

I feel minuscule as I pass underneath,
marvel at architectural majesty,
wonder how such massive heights were reached
without today's technology
that knows no bounds

I pause before carved figures,
Peter, Michael, Paul,
Jesus on His cross,
imagine dedicated carvers
pouring their passion
into their craft

Visualize monks
in their silent, reverent routines,
believe I hear their robes swish
as they walk cloistered arcade,
sure I hear bells calling them to vespers

Arcade stands empty now,
roofless walls stand guard
over empty walkways,
crows and tourists
your only visitors anymore

Still, just behind the veil
that thinly separates my world from theirs
I can hear monks whisper,
feel their spirits floating
among arches and open windows,
communing with any who turn their way

Cobh, Titanic Horizon

Harbor streets
lined with brilliant colored homes
physical rainbow of houses
red, blue, yellow, green,
all vivid, gay

It's easy to forget
you once graced this harbor,
too large to enter all the way,
forced to float on outer edge
as mail and passengers
were ferried out to you

Your last stop,
last glimpse of land
your passengers would see

I stand on sidewalk by shore
White Star Line office visible to me
gaze at horizon
imagine I can see you there,
beautiful lady
magnificent jewel

Turn back to gaily painted houses,
now blurred by my tears
for all that was lost with you

Walking St. Ciarán's Ground

Spirits speak
through silent air,
across decades and centuries,
draw the faithful and the curious
to walk green fields
where stone on stone stand testament
to another era
where faith was the power
that shaped men's lives,
where the monastery was central
and saints the leaders of the day.

I walk with reverence,
heart attuned to the words you might whisper,
grateful to be in your presence.
Walk the round,
you instruct at the base
of the capless tower,
feel the circular
which always carries strength.
I walk,
feel smoothness and continuity,
contemplate their places in my life
where so many hard edges cut and tear.

I kneel at the base of your holy high cross.
I don't notice if anyone else does,
I don't care.
It's a movement I need to make.

A hundred high crosses stand testimony
to a time when faith was tangible.
It slips out of sight in our present age
where so many hurl their way through days
too chaotic to make sense of,
too complex to navigate,
faith eroding in a lost world,
tilting like so many stone slabs and crosses
that once stood here firm,
disintegrating like so many stone walls.

I cry for St. Ciarán to return.

Stepping Through The Open Gate

Small black gate
swung open in stone wall
beckons me to step up, walk through.

I climb ancient steps,
traverse wall,
walk green field to water's edge,

Ponder how many times
life offers open gates to walk through,
stone walls to traverse,

How many chances
to step into unknown,
experience new, overcome.

Green field feels soft under my feet,
grass springs back
from where I have stepped.

Indelible tracks cross my heart,
leave their stamp
of courage rewarded.

Pilgrim, Fatigued

One foot in front of another
Journey on over rocky roads
Paths too narrow to walk two abreast

Legs scratched from thorny shrubs
Feet and back aching
Map blurred by steady falling rain

Foes attacking, berating,
Throwing boulders
Antagonizing at every turn

Aedh arrived at Clonmacnoise
Exhausted,
Collapsed at monastery gates

I struggle
To remain on life's path
Enemies rushing at every side

I can only shield my eyes
From world gone so far astray
From my own weak failings

No monastery to shelter me
End of the road still
So very far away

Shannon River's Edge

Cross green field
to stand at your edge,
holy river of Ireland

water laps gently at grassy shore,
gentle waves from fishing boats
cause rippled reflection

I marvel at the history
these fields have felt cross,
this river has witnessed

ancient kings holding court,
great tribal shows of power and wealth,

warring parties rushing in
to plunder and maim,

naïve volunteers
taking up the battle for freedom,

destitute farmers
falling, starved, on your banks.

Their voices echo
across wind brushed grass,
mix with trees' rustling leaves,
whisper their tales.

A swan slides across
smooth waters,
a child of Lir, I wonder,
separated from her companions?

I slip my hand into your magical waters,
draw healing out and bless myself.
I am now connected to you,
another part of your story.

Joe Kelly's World

Nestled in pastures
near Shannon River's run
Joe Kelly's world plays out
with ritual regularity
serving breakfasts,
cleaning house,
preparing for the next night's guests.

Summer fills his house with travelers,
local monastic ruins a magnetic draw.
Days pass quickly filling needs,
answering questions,
keeping all in line.

Autumn traffic slows,
the odd guest here and there
as leaves turn bronze and gold,
summer flowers fade to memory,
sunset earlier, sunrise later,
preparations completed for the season ahead.

Winter falls hard on Joe Kelly's home,
not in snowfall but in darkness,
hearth fire warms and brightens
long winter nights,
television a welcome companion,
coffee with neighbors or trips to the pub
a frequent diversion.

Spring brings respite from solitary world,
renewal of leaf and flower,
cows returning to pasture nearby,
stock is taken, fresh round of supplies set in
and travelers return to find warmth and welcome
in Joe Kelly's world.

Himself

He stands at bar
in neighborhood pub
regales regulars with stories
some have heard fifty times over
yet they nod and laugh
at appropriate points anyway.
He greets visitors with a nod
and perhaps a hello
joins the lads at the end of the bar in a song
his fingers dancing across guitar strings
with familiarity
albeit hesitantly with the slowness
that comes with age
his voice still strong
as he sings a song of loss
and heartache that seems
so intensely personal
I want to ask him the story
behind the song
yet I hold back,
some things are better left unasked.
He nurses a pint and then another
and a third
drawing them out so they last through the night
and perhaps this time
he will return home
a little more sober.
Still he is slightly inebriated
when he walks through his front door
the house all too quiet
lager softening the hard edges of life
for another night
he reclines in armchair
where he has slept ever since Her passing
the bed they shared far too empty
for any sleep now.
Tomorrow
and the next night
and the one after
he will repeat his routine.

West Cork Cottage

Papers crinkle under my feet,
and bits of dried leaves
and paint droppings,
as I step inside,
poor refuge from the
driving rain with rivulets
stealing in through holey roof,
sliding down peeled paint.
Moldy watermarks stain your walls
new colors, new patterns.
Chipped scraps of china grace
your window table, not worth
the cost of disposal, but
they were once somebody's treasures,
as were the washed out photos
that lie in a corner heap,
the odd dresses hanging in the
bedroom wardrobe, dust drenched,
spider webbed,
the old boots fallen by the hearth.
I would buy this abandoned cottage
if I could,
repair its holes,
repaint its walls,
fill it with light and laughter,
music and life
as it once knew so long ago.

They Once Were Kings and Queens

Young woman barefoot
long hair covered in hand crocheted shawl
basket of turf beside her
toddlers begging food of her
as she stirs a pot over hearth fire

her head held high
regal neck, prideful eyes
she knows she is of royal lineage
descended from kings and queens of old

as is the dairy farmer
guiding his meager herd along country roads
threadbare shirt
shoes with leather worn through
his polite nod does not condescend
nor does it submit.

They know their heritage
the royal blood that flows through their veins
surnames as ancient as the land they traverse,
the kings and queens,
warriors and lords who ruled long before them

far cry from the lives they lead now
no castles, no army to serve them
no land to defend.

They carry on
know they are better than what they seem
hold that secret close
inside shawl and jacket
gather turf, clean barns, plow fields
refuse to acknowledge defeat
refuse to surrender their hearts.

A Widow's Christmas

She places candle in cottage window,
one lone weak light
to guide the Christ child
to her tiny abode,
empty now save for herself.
Two sons departed for America,
please God they will have arrived there safe
although she knows she may not hear
for a long time.
Rumors swirl of thousands dying
on outbound ships,
pray her two are not among them.
Husband recently passed on
to the next world,
may his soul rest in peace.
She turns to his chair in the corner
grown cold,
wonders why she bothers to light candle now,
there is no one left for the Christ Child to bless
and she with not so much as a cup of tea
or biscuit to offer Him should He stop by.
Still she leaves candle in window,
reclines on bed and drifts to sleep
dreaming of Christmases past,
wakes to find soup on the hearth,
cake on the table,
tea to be brewed,
wonders what neighbor has visited,
knows none of her neighbors has any to spare
or even enough to stave off hunger themselves.
The soup has meat,
there's sugar for tea
and a letter to her
though no post would have come.
She wonders what grace has visited her,
crosses herself and gives thanks to God
sure a miracle has been granted.

Salthill Solace

Tired feet
After long day's work
Step onto beach
Seek refreshment of spirit
In sound of water on shore
In feel of soft sand beneath shoes

Weight of world
Bears down on shoulders
Relationship failed
Finances stretched to tearing
Dreams lying dormant
While you try to navigate reality
Shoes move heavy over sand
Spirit sags
Buffeted by Atlantic wind

Until in distance
Sound of calls and cheers rises
Children climb over rocks
Splash each other with ocean's waters
Sunlight reflecting copper
And bronze off hair
Lightness of play carried
through laughter on breeze

Steps move lighter now across sand
Play tag with encroaching waves
Cast off burdens
That bowed shoulders
Far too long

Irish Rain

Sometimes soft,
like the Shannon's gentle flow
across green fields,

sometimes hard,
like Connemara's
rock strewn mountains,

rain will fall in Ireland.
It's where the green
rises from.

An almost daily occurrence,
it seeps into your bones
and tries to drench your spirit.

Do Not
let it settle
into your heart!

Fight back!
Force yourself
to stroll windswept beaches,

to find light
in stores
and coffee shops,

to seek out gardens
and sheep dotted fields
and deep blue loughs,

to find the sun
in the places in your heart
where it still shines.

Cottage By The Sea

If you had not taken me in
offered me a room in your home
I would never have known hope
or that sunrise could be so beautiful
or nightfall so glorious
I would never have thought
I could contribute anything good
to the world around me
or that I had anything good in me
at all
I would have missed the sight
of herons fishing at the edge of our sea
or otters playing by the rocks
at shore's edge
or soft days in our gardens
where the fuschia tree still amuses me
I would have given up on life
if you had not opened your arms
and your house
and invited me in

Rosmuc, Summer's Eve

Quiet,
Water's lapping against stone shore,
Whisper of breeze through summer leaves,
Robin's cheery call

Solitude
Of space and time,
Sunlight glistening off gentle waves,
Peaceful heart and mind at rest

Oh man of many burdens,
Weight of a nation bowing strong shoulders,
Heart crying for a culture and people
So long abandoned they are nearly lost,

How welcome
Rosmuc summer
Must have been,
City pressures left behind,

Nothing
But sweet ocean scent
And calm Connemara countryside
To nurture body and soul

Cleggan

Wild Atlantic wind
beat against my window
all through the night,
howling like spirits long gone
still wanting to be part of our world

I could picture the waves crashing
near Omey, where you live,
exceptional view
but no easy place this,
gorgeous in sunlight
but wild Atlantic wind batters
and humbles

Morning rain
slashes against window pane,
cascades down,
turf fire and hot tea bring comfort.

Under Mweelrea's Shadow

Giants must have formed you,
walked your high ridgeback
as if it were child's play,
sure they could touch the sun
from your great height.

Overpowering my view,
I feel tiny in your shadow,
awed by your dimensions,
almost frozen by your majesty,

Watch rivulets stream down your side,
silver-white veins bleeding water
into streams that nourish vegetation
which feed mountainside sheep
that nourish and clothe us.

Ribbon of road
that passes at Mweelrea's base
seems an afterthought,
a slender thread the giants painted
on grand canvas.

Behind Benbulben

Staring at your face
through window over morning breakfast
I know I must move forward
put yesterday's struggles behind me
although I am still afraid
still haunted by what went wrong
the day before

I bundle myself into car
and drive on
take careful turns towards
my next destination

road leads to your back side
Dartry Mountains stunning landscape
high green embankments
with weather carved scars along top

Evergreen patches
and shades of light red
mix with grey stone and green grass
as you sweep down to grey-blue lough

I wonder how many centuries
how many millions of years
you were in the making

And I realize
behind Benbulben
is a sight I would never have seen
if I'd stayed frozen
by yesterday's fear and failures.

Drumcliffe Night

Vantage point
high above your bay,
I watch Drumcliffe ease into night,

shadow of clouds
grows deeper grey
against watercolor blue sky,

colors dim,
sun turns to pink gold

beneath your smoky blue mountains,
cottage houses turn lights on
one by one

amber stars
against evening dark.

I think of Brigadoon
appearing by magic,
think this view just as mystical,

close my eyes for sleep
and wonder
if the magic will hold

and you will still be here
come morning.

Carrowmore, Veil Lifted

Walk with reverence
across your grassy field,
feel your spirits rise
through sun-warmed grounds,
listen hard to hear your message
carried over breeze
that bends and tosses wildflowers
scattered like stars among
blanket of green,

Five thousand year old voices
call to me from beneath
stone circles and burial chambers,
I try to understand,
try to decipher ancient carving,
weather worn, faintly visible,

Try to fathom reason for placement,
openings aligned with February
and November morning sun,
circle laid out at irregular intervals,
meaning unknown to me now,

Still I hear your whispers,
feel your spirits tug at me,
thin space where veil
between your world and mine
is almost non-existent,

Believe the meaning of stones
is not as complex as we make it,
your circles and chambers
less mysterious code,
more labor of love,
markers to remember
those who have passed,
those you loved, those you mourned,

We use crosses and headstones
you used boulders and circles,
we are, perhaps,
not so different after all.

Strong As Stone

How many hands did it take
to build this stone wall
that stretches as far as my eye can see?
How many years
of clearing rock strewn fields,
harvest of boulders more bountiful
than any crop you tried to grow?

Set at irregular angles,
I wonder how this wall stands at all,
how it has stood so many decades,
no nails, no wire,
how gale force winds have not
shifted it or worn it down.

Spirit inside you endures
as strong as any stone walls
that crisscross your country.
Vikings and Normans could not tame you,
neither famine nor persecution
diminish your will to survive,
your ability to overcome.

Even your remnants,
fragments of castles and houses
wind and time could not erase,
fragments of families
cast to the earth's four corners,
prove your ability to endure,
your heart and stamina.

How strong the hands
that raised this stone wall.
How strong the spirit
that never could be broken.

Late Night Blue

Late night blue,
all I see as I stand on shore,
waves, shore and sky combined
in similar shades, all blue
that match my lonely heart.
Waves break on rocks at my feet,
expanse of water that separates us,
each wave break whispers your name,
holy word too sacred to breathe out loud,
or is that only the call of my heart?

Lighthouse beam penetrates landscape,
sweeps across blue sea,
searches for you,
returns to home base and tries again.
Light of day will send us both home empty,
but now, at night, I stand on shore,
peer deep into blue landscape,
hear your name whispered on waves,
echoed in air,
wait for your return.

Love Among Ruins

They played
among crumbling walls,
daughter of kings
son of farmers

their shadows blending
with shadow of high crosses,
carved figures on abbey walls
watching in silence

whether mocking or shocked
they never knew,
carved figures whisper no secrets
stone faces offer no judgment

as play turned to romance
shadowy figures clasped behind round towers,
hidden by headstones
embraces turned frantic

movements as rhythmic
as the rush of waves
of ocean and sand meeting

and parting.

Secret exposed,

army of warriors
rushing through field,
eyes fixed on singular subject,
sword glinting in sun

Farmer's son
lying on empty field
as warriors depart,
daughter of kings
watches from window
hiding her tears
as father looks on.

Under Cottage Eaves

In his bed
I feel safe,
tucked into his gentle embrace,
his whispers calm and comfort,
his strong arms
my security

We fit into
each other's needs
like well-matched hook and eye,
taste each other's passion,
respond to each other's urging

Until, spent,
we lie in comfortable silence,
no pressure,
no awkward break

As natural as if
we had always been meant
for each other.

Lough Derg Boat

Quiet lough,
retired boat by its side,
I pulled my car close,
shut its engine down,
stepped outside to a rock
calling me to rest with it.
Soft blue waters
lapped gently at shore,
song birds told me their secrets,
their loves,
the concerns that filled my mind
slipped away
one by one,
my shoulders relaxed,
my pulse slowed,
I stayed by this lough,
this boat,
until sunlight started
to slide towards water
and evening called me home.

Antique Lace

I

She sits in corner
long after her family has gone to bed,
turf fire casting odd shadows against stone walls
that would have caused her fear
had she time to pay them any mind,
but these days time is her taskmaster
as she hurries to finish her work,
needle moving through netted frame with deft speed
forming a pattern in her mind's eye,
the stitches she learned from her grandmother,
the design is one of her own
based on the singular line of roses
that crawls up the trellis outside her cottage.
In her haste she pricks her finger,
rose red droplets spreading across calloused skin
so quickly she drops her work to the ground,
blood stains would never do
on this most special piece of clothing.

II

Any fine lady would pay a high price indeed
for this hand crafted lace dress,
exquisite in detail,
each stitch so perfect
as to be from a machine
should such a stitching machine exist.
The most powerful magnifying glass
would find no fault here,
nor would the pattern be matched anywhere,
a unique one of a kind treasure
that would surely fetch the highest price,
yet this dress was made for no fine lady.
It would be for her daughter
who should have something grand on her wedding day.
The years ahead as a farmer's wife

would be hard enough,
no luxury to them.
Sure, love would carry her through,
and a passel of children riches enough.
Still, this elegant dress
for this one special day
was the finest gift she could give,
never mind what price would be offered at market,
and her own cupboard bare
as the feet of her own young ones.
The light in her daughter's eyes
when she slips this wedding dress on
would be worth any sacrifice.

III

The dress now hangs in a lace museum
freshly laundered,
white as new snow and just as clean scented,
no frayed edges or tears
to mar its pristine beauty.
Visitors examine the dress,
invent stories of princesses
who surely would have owned such finery,
or manor house ladies
who would have worn this treasure
to summer tea parties,
delicate white floating over a sea of green lawn
or drifting among lavender and delphinium
in a vast garden.
They imagine the diamonds and pearls
that would have graced the curved neckline,
the alabaster skin that would have carried the dress,
never dreaming
the country wedding at which it first appeared
a hundred years ago,
or its tissue wrapped shelter
in a dresser drawer
in a farm house just miles down the road.

Finding Warmth in Caroline's Kitchen

Enniskillen too rain-soaked,
grey and cold,
and me alone and having no stomach
to brave a depressing city,
I traveled a few miles down the road,

told myself all I wanted was a hot cup of tea,
knew I was lying to myself,
I wanted more comfort than that

Caroline's Kitchen appeared
and I stopped in,
found tea and brown stew
and so much more,
Caroline's bright smile
to chase away my blues,
she taking time out
for a cup of tea with me,

Greeting youth as they stopped in
on their way home from school,
chatting with patrons who came by
for coffee and brownies,
pulse of the community
running through her store,
compassion and care
offered freely for all,

I would have loved
to spend the day in her
bright yellow room,
taking tea and pastries
before the turf fire,
chatting with her
but, my spirit restored,
the road called me
and I traveled on.

Lough Erne Remembered

Drive around your gentle shores,
soft blue waters
laced with soft green trees,
dotted with myriad islands,

I find no place
to stop and take your picture.

Some things
cannot be physically held forever,
the image of white swans
floating on your surface,
white tower at the edge
of one of your islands,

but only carried in the mind
and heart the rest of my days.

Mary By The Water

Eyes closed
you stand in perpetual prayer
for the souls laid to eternal rest
at your feet
for those of us
still walking this earth

Wind buffets your robe
erodes stone wall behind you
lichen stains mantle brown and rust
bruises your face and arms

You pay no heed
stand firm
unshaken
unmovable

In a world turned upside down
buffeted by gale winds
drowned by storms
no solid ground at our feet
faith a dwindling commodity

So many turning away
in the face of controversy
so hard to hear your voice
above this world's constant din

I bow before you
pray your serenity
will calm my soul
your strength
will override my weakness
your faithfulness
will steady my path

Irish Rainbows

I think God must have given you
an extra portion of beauty
restitution for the double portion
of heartache and suffering
you've been dealt
through the ages
brilliant sunshine to wash over
your all too frequent rains
arches of color
connecting heaven to earth
to remind you
hard times eventually pass

Donegal Castle Ghosts

Everywhere I step
as I tour your magnificent castle
refurbished rooms spotless,
minimally appointed,
sunshine gleaming through windows
casting pale gold shadows
on smooth, immaculate floors,

Every place I enter
in your immaculate home
I hear your whispers,
feel your spirits pull at my heart,
imagine you walking these boards,
taking meals at this table,
relaxing in these chairs

Visualize your agonized decision
to depart from the country you loved,
Flight of the Earls,
end of Gaelic order,
cringe at the thought of
your enemies making your home their own
cry at the sight of the
Annals of the Four Masters manuscript
in your display case,
compilation of ancient Irish history
ended all too soon

Light in your windows
comforts me, gives me hope
even as I leave your spirit
and your whispers behind

Transfixed At Slieve League

So far above
steel blue Atlantic waters
I cannot hear waves whisper
or crash against your rocks below,
can only stand, transfixed,
and watch their wind driven movement,
miles of ripples spread out before me,
changing direction
where currents meet,
shining silver patches
where weak sun casts its light.

Brown-grey rocks
rise in graduated heights
from water bed,
strong and proud,
as old as time,
shaped by wind and ages,
captivating,
drawing me to read
their multicolored surfaces,
memorize their shapes and lines,
understand them,
know them.

Lowering sun
breaks through clouds,
casts golden light
on grey-brown rocks,
sets them afire
in glorious oranges and yellows,
transforms them as if by magic,
illuminating horseshoe heart of coastline,
aqua patches of water,
slip of sandy shore
impossible to reach on foot.

Cara Na Mara, Magheraclogher

Strong wind and rain drive everyone inside
except me.
I grab window of opportunity
to stroll sandy shores,
my only company the odd seagull,
a scattering of shells,
waves encroaching from Atlantic
as tide returns home,
Mount Errigal watching me
from its high perch behind cottages,

and you,
Cara Na Mara
Friend of the Sea,
weather worn, wind battered,
wood slowly returning to air and soil.

Surprised to find you share my beach,
I approach,
place a light hand on your evaporating shoulders,
a blessing,
a fingered kiss.
Your disintegration may be complete
when next I walk these shores.

Wind blows harder now,
rain sets in again.
I leave you to Errigal's watchful eye
and seagull's occasional return.

Crossing Derryveagh Mountains

Don't think me strong
that I have traversed
so great a mass of mountains,
that I have guided my car successfully
over narrow, winding roads

My scars are well hidden,
my trembling hands
held at rest before your eyes

You do not know
how I begged God
to not send me over these heights,
fear turning knees to jelly,
stomach turning somersaults,
tears blinding map before me

I traveled forth anyway,
one does what one must,
but do not think me brave or strong.
Each turn of the wheel
I have grasped God's hand
and pled mercy.

Fine Mist, Clearing

Fine mist veils the shoreline
and hills outside my car
as I drive this empty road,
narrow grooves worn
through grass and stone,
gorse blooming golden on either side,
dove grey sky overhead,
if I open my windows
I would hear songbirds call
but I choose to remain alone with my thoughts,
peaceful silence the brass ring I grab,
so many thoughts to sort through,
past to let go of,
future to arrange.
Inside my home these thoughts
all jumble together
like the stack of laundry,
sink full of dishes,
constant blare of tv or radio,
impossible atmosphere
in which to order my mind.

Fine mist and soft, open landscape
clear confusion away,
nourish my heart and mind,
I feed on gentle rolling waves,
solitary footprints
along the empty beach I choose,
conversation with the lone gull
who sweeps down,
offers a word of advice
and wheels away,
water color mirroring
the expanse overhead
until my mind and heart
mirror sky and water's
smooth, soft surface.

Two Cottages

Both stand empty among
Deserted fields
On lonely mountain road

Abandoned by
Impoverished farmers
Or deceased inhabitants
Victims of hunger or
Famine related disease

Their voices cry
Out to me from
Empty windows, unopened
Doors, holes in
Weather worn roofs

No one left to
Care for fields, to
Tend to repairs,
Two cottages stand forlorn,
Haunt the rest
Of my drive,

Linger on my
Mind the same way they
Linger on landscape,
Grey-brown stone
Upon stone

Worn tree
Between them standing
Silent guard

Five Hundred Ploughs

What a strange sight they made
on the rare section of road
that had a wide shoulder

Plough after plough
heading home
after national championship

Neatly lined
one after another
some solo, some with children riding
alongside driver

Throwbacks to an era
I no longer see where I live

As are towns so small
one road defines them

And clear vistas
with no billboards to mar them

And skies full of stars
not drowned by city lights

I envisioned plough hands returning home
to well tended fields
cleaning their ploughs
after the long rain soaked journey

Then settling before a turf fire
hot cup of tea in hand
children's chatter filling the spaces around them

Blue Stack Mountain Pass

Weight of you
pins Ireland to earth,
tips balance heavy toward west
where bands of rain
sweep in from Atlantic Ocean,
deposit their water load
then head back out for more

Roads too narrow and rough
to camera capture
your majestic beauty,
coal grey hulking shoulders
shrugging off wind and rain,
defending eastern counties
from marauding weather

I wonder how many
warriors, rebels, freedom fighters
sheltered in your bracken,
nestled among your trees and shrubs,
foraged for food,
struggled for survival

High terrain
would have made a perfect refuge,
rocks and sheep
would never give them away.

Grianan At Night

Clear night.
Milky Way strewn across sky
more blue than black
like diamonds draped
against a queen's throat

Moonlight searches out shadows
slipping between sheaves of hay
invaders stealing in from the north.

Grianan
deceptively quiet
watches as steadfast as
celestial lights

Waits for marauding bands
to reach foot of the mountain
upon which she stands.

Then she will show them!
Her horsemen will thunder out
catch marauders off guard
teach them she and her inhabitants
are no easy prey!

She is dreaming.
Invaders no longer sweep through fields
there are no more kings to protect
no treasures to secret away
no villagers to lend her safe walls to.

Still she stands her ground
majestic in her three tiered strength
noble in her steadfast height

She keeps watchful eye
over fields and loughs spread below her
laughs at rain and thunder
and wind that try to uproot her
winks at stars that shimmer above
believes they will not outlast her.

Song For Derry

Evening sky
shines golden above you,
light through the clouds,
barrier against darkness,
illuminating you
as a gallery light
illuminates a treasure.

Gold you are.
St. Columcille knew this,
treasure of God,
city of blessings
that shine through the shadows.
Nighttime cannot hold you,
your beauty will always shine forth.

I carry your gold in my heart
in the smiles of your people,
in the songs of your music,
in your artists and writers,
buildings and walls.
Your light shines hope to me,
candle glowing in night,
shining in your city's windows
until I return.

Bloody Sunday Revisited

Truth,
as hard to decipher
as your complex Celtic knots,
where does one side start
and the other one end?

But Celtic knots *can* be deciphered,
and so can truth,
after time,
after passion's flames cool
and fresh eyes take a measured view,
cut away embellishments,
weigh fact and reason,
in the end truth is laid bare,
accepted.

Bittersweet,
so many years denied,
justice proclaimed cannot bring life
to buried bones,
undo wounds and scars
that run so deep;

but finally names are cleared,
and you can hold your head up high
in the market square,
knowing that, at last,
the knot has been unraveled,
the world knows what is true.

Bishop Street Without

I can only imagine
how hard the struggle must have been
day after day
crowded quarter living
in the shadow of great stone walls,
the division that marked
those welcomed, protected,
from those outcast

Abuse heaped upon abuse
by those with supplanted pedigree
upon those whose roots were true
landlord upon tenant,
aristocrat upon laborer
Christian upon Christian

Until the smoldering fire of indignities
burst into flame,
well past time to fight back,
demand proper treatment,
demand justice and respect

I can only imagine the shouts of anger
rumble of armored vehicles
clatter of tear gas canisters,
click of rifles, blast of car bombs

Until too many lie dead.
Hard to declare who won
too many innocents lost
(although innocents must sometimes
be sacrificed in battles for justice).

Even now great wall
seems too clear a divide
between those with plenty
and those who struggle to make ends meet,
unresolved tensions
simmering just below surface.
Pray peace holds fast
wonder how long it can
when so many still live in shadow.

A Gathering of Friends

Just a small place, really,
a handful of tables,
a bar, a bank of windows.
Forty people here would be a crowd.
Fairy lights intertwine among
rows of glasses, on light fixtures,
skulls and skeletons mix
with rebel posters and memorabilia.

I enter, a stranger,
and am soon wrapped
in the same blanket of warmth
that shields others here
against the damp chill
of the world outside these walls.

Conversations flow
as freely as pints and wine consumed,
this person still searching for jobs,
that one's latest heartbreak,
the passing of one's friend,
celebration for another's promotion,

and I understand
this place is less about beverages consumed
and more about people,
a gathering of friends,
a welcoming home.

Other End Of The Bridge

So long trying to eke out a living
In this grey town
Thick walls surrounding the centre
Thick walls surrounding my heart
Each day a struggle inside and out

If I stay my sorrow will swallow me
If I escape I leave behind all I have known
No easy choice here
Only heartache as thick
As the grey fog that hides
The other end of this bridge

No guaranties
That the other side of that fog
Will bring sunshine
Or fortune
Or even an easier day

To do nothing
To stay where I am
Is unacceptable to me
Inertia a trap that will bind me here
Far too long

I point my car towards invisible bridge end
Sure at the very least
The road will continue
Beyond the fog cloud

White Wine and Smiles

I see twinkles in your eyes
not pain
although I know pain has visited
more deeply than some of us
may guess

you hide that from the
world at large
carry on day after day
one foot in front of the other

always focusing on what
others may need
always working to create
a better world

I see your photos from
childhood and
university days
see your bright smiles
your joy

that has not faded

you tell me stories
over white wine and
sparkling water
allow me to enter
part of your world

a treasure more priceless
than any my travels
could have garnered

you are the hardest things
for me to leave behind

Soft Days

Soft rain leaks down
From soft grey skies
Does not drench
But refreshes in its own odd way

Soft days
After so many years of struggle
To reach a place
Where one's time passes
In pints and casual conversations

Soft partings
No more tears
Only resolution that separate paths
Are necessary
Not easy
But no longer tearing the heart

Pigeons fly over the city
As I pull my car away
Pray for soft blessings
On those I leave behind

Crossing Carrick-a-Rede

Swallow my fears
as I descend steep stairs
to your slender bridge,
more steel than rope now
but still fearsome
dangling eighty feet
over jagged rocks and sea.

I have determined
I would cross you,
cast my fear of heights aside,
trust your tethered sides would hold,
would not let me die.

View from island side astounds me,
lone cottage clinging to edge,
gulls sheltering on cliffside nests
brown/black seaweed
under aqua waters
glistening as sun shines crystals on them,
phosphorescent green arch in rock cave.

Mesmerized,
I could stay island-side for hours,
descend treacherous steps down
to cottage and beg a cup of tea,
study waterfowl feeding in groups
on water's glass-smooth surface,
drink in your splendor
until dark of night
would force me home.

Lost in Mussenden Temple

Milky Way glistens above us,
a million jewels I have called upon
to celebrate your presence here,
our time together,
Aurora Borealis tinges twilight
hints of green and red,
celestial fireworks to commemorate
our passion, our love.
Let others think this solitary temple
a library, a haven for learning,
a quiet place to ponder world-weighty issues,
although some will have guessed my true motive,
this rendezvous point, this trysting place
perched on cliff edge,
Atlantic's soothing waves below,
sky and sea spread wide before us,
endless field of possibilities
upon which our dreams can be cast
as a fisherman casts a net,
no guaranties, no promises,
only two souls joined by one united heart.

I know we will be found out in the end,
will have to part ways,
one of us to distant shores
to prevent our further union,
but tonight Milky Way
shines down on our love,
your skin as soft as the jasmine air
that drifts our way from nearby garden,
our love-making as thunderous as the waves below
crashing against shore to announce a coming storm,
your curves as smooth
as the curve of wall and ceiling
in this haven of love,
this solitary refuge.

I am lost in you.
I am lost without you.
Let this temple stand forever
as testament to what we once had.

Causeway Reflection

Irregular field of hexagon columns
stretches hundreds of yards before me
try to pick my way
over them without twisting a foot
amazed to see sea pinks
blooming in cracks among the columns
wildflowers do find a way
to survive in the narrowest crevices

Such an odd, other-worldly panorama,
field of imagination
as I search out pipe organ,
granny, camel, and boot,
sit on wishing chair,
climb highest peak,
absorb landscape surrounding me

Sound of waves smooth, soothing
against irregular shore,
I step over columns to water's edge,
let wave spray splash upon me
panic when tide rushes in
and water level raises higher,
afraid I will not make it back to safe ground
in time

Sun dips lower on horizon as I leave,
rays of light reflect off water
like a million sequins sparkling
against dark background
brilliant pools of silver
contrasting with black rocks,
captivating, unforgettable.

Ravens Circling Overhead

Like some dark spirits
lurking over their domain,
ravens circle high over Ireland,
perching on the tall peak
ruins at Dunluce Castle,
nesting in the open topped
round tower at Clonmacnoise,
guarding Jerpoint's empty walkways,
hovering over abandoned cottages
and silent fields,
and I wonder what
they have come to steal off her next,
this hard land, this people
who have known such loss,
what they have come to curse now,
what bones can be left to
pick the flesh off of.
Sure the ravens must know
what lies below the surface,
that this country,
these people,
will always rise again,
proud, determined, undefeated.

Fair Head Light

So easy to lose my way
down multiple roads,
narrow lanes with high hedges
impossible to see my way clear of,
winding, twisted roads
with so many blind ascents,
no way to anticipate and prepare for next curve,
sheep and stone walls my only landmarks,
and both so multiple I am easily confused

Fair Head light
still glows red at night,
pulsating flashes guide me safely
around jagged rocks,
dangerous coasts,
morning will find me safely home.

A Song of Ireland

I know a song of Ireland,
of yellow canola fields
and golden gorse,
of rocky shores
and crashing waves,
and castles rising up
from grassy knolls.

I know a song of Ireland,
of ancient kings
and legendary giants,
of mountain roads
and city walls
and weathered,
crumbling cottages.

If I know a song of Ireland,
does Ireland know a song of me?
Of where my feet trod her soil,
where my hands
caressed her castle walls?
Of where my heart rose
with her soaring shorebirds?

Does Ireland recall
where I walked along her rivers,
where I let her ocean
wash my feet,
where I trembled
climbing ancient steps,
and where I failed to climb?

I know a song of Ireland,
of ancestors
fighting to be free,
of dreamers
seeking a better world.
Does Ireland hear
the song of my heart
seeking to return
to her gentle rolling hills?

Ireland Dawn

Soft grey fills the view
Outside my bedroom window
As the morning and I come awake

No brilliant sunrise here
Only subtle shadings
As gentle as the room I inhabit
Safe, peaceful womb
In which I have sheltered
After another long traveling day

View over pastureland
Turns from deep to mid-grey
From mid to lighter color
As pleasant as only pasturelands can know
No city lights or harsh noises
To disturb song of birds
Or easy stirrings of cows and sheep

Somewhere over Ireland today
Storms will break
Rain will fall over mountains and towns
Wind driven rains buffet rocks and beaches
Yet this pasture and I
Will remain at peace.

Upon Leaving Dublin

How fitting
That rain should fall
As I travel to airport
Clouds unleashing
The great flow of tears
Spilling over from my heart

Ensconced in great Airbus
Gravity's bonds are cut
One last look is offered
Of patchwork tans and greens
Rural fields dotted with roads and loughs

Until clouds drift in
To sever my ties
With strangers become friends
And bed and breakfasts deemed home

Home is now two places
And I stand
One foot set on each

Acknowledgements

I am grateful, first and foremost, to Beth Bales Ostrowski. Without you my first dream trip to Ireland would never have happened, and this book would not exist. Thank you for sharing my dream, and all the laughs and fun along the way. As always, thank you too for your excellent artwork. How you know what I want before I even say it is beyond me, but you always do know! I am grateful to a number of friends in Ireland who have helped make my visits there, and particularly my most recent trip, so pleasant - Caroline, Hilary, Cathal and Siona, Joe, Joan and Caryll, and Finola, thank you for the blessings and the special memories. Dermie and Pauline, thank you hardly expresses my gratitude and deep affection for you both. Thank you so much for sharing your time and stories with me. Reaching for dreams is not always easy; I am thankful for friends and family who encourage and support me along the way.

Made in the USA
Las Vegas, NV
11 December 2021